CHILI

CHILI

INTRODUCTION BY JENNY FLEETWOOD

southwater

This edition is published by Southwater

Southwater is an imprint of
Anness Publishing Limited
Hermes House
88–89 Blackfriars Road
London SE1 8HA
tel. 020 7401 2077
fax 020 7633 9499

Distributed in the UK by
The Manning Partnership
251–253 London Road East
Batheaston
Bath BA1 7RL
tel. 01225 852 727
fax 01225 852 852

Distributed in the USA by
Anness Publishing Inc.
27 West 20th Street
Suite 504
New York
NY 10011
tel. 212 807 6739
fax 212 807 6813

Distributed in Australia by
Sandstone Publishing
Unit 1
360 Norton Street
Leichhardt
New South Wales 2040
tel. 02 9560 7888
fax 02 9560 7488

1 3 5 7 9 10 8 6 4 2

Publisher Joanna Lorenz
Senior Cookery Editor Linda Fraser
Project Editor Anne Hildyard
Designer Bill Mason
Illustrations Anna Koska

Photographers Karl Adamson, Edward Allwright, David Armstrong, Steve Baxter, James Duncan,
Michelle Garrett, Amanda Heywood, Patrick McLeavey and Thomas Odulate
Recipes Carla Capalbo, Frances Cleary, Elizabeth Wolf-Cohen, Nicola Diggins, Rafi Fernandez, Sarah Gates,
Shirley Gill, Deh-Ta Hsiung, Shehzad Husain, Sallie Morris, Liz Trigg and Steven Wheeler
Food for photography Frances Cleary, Elizabeth Wolf-Cohen, Carole Handslip, Jane Hartshorn,
Wendy Lee, Jane Stevenson and Steven Wheeler
Stylists Maria Kelly and Blake Minton

For all recipes, quantities are given in both metric and imperial measures and, where appropriate,
measures are also given in standard cups and spoons. Follow one set, but not a mixture,
because they are not interchangeable.

Previously published as *Cooking with Chilies*

Contents

INTRODUCTION

Powerhouses of flavour and fire, chillies are wonderful ingredients, well worth exploring in all their many and varied forms. Their reputation as one of the hottest properties on the culinary scene is undoubtedly well deserved, but what is equally true (and perhaps less fully appreciated) is that they can also be subtle. Add a whole chilli when cooking a casserole or stew, remove it at the end, and you introduce the merest flicker of flame. To turn up the heat slightly, use sliced medium-hot chillies, defusing them somewhat by scraping out the seeds. Later, if your courage (and your constitution) will stand it, go for the burn by cooking with the hottest varieties, leaving the seeds in.

Chillies are native to Central and Southern America and were a well-kept secret for centuries. It is said that the Aztec emperor Montezuma insisted on having thirty different dishes prepared for him every evening, many of them spiced with one or more of the dozens of varieties of chilli available. When the Spanish conquistadores arrived in the sixteenth century, they were struck by how delicious the local food was, and gold was not the only treasure they took with them when they sailed for home.

Europeans embraced chillies – and their mild-mannered relations, the sweet bell peppers – with great enthusiasm, and within a very short time they had also been introduced to Asia. Today, they add their distinctive flavour to dishes as diverse as Indian, Malaysian and Thai curries, Indonesian rijstafel, Hungarian goulash and Austrian paprika schnitzel. In France, that innocuous-looking but lively red mayonnaise that accompanies bouillabaisse is spiked with chillies.

Mexico continues to furnish some of the most exciting and innovative recipes for this magical ingredient. With so many varieties at their disposal, Mexican cooks will often use two types of chilli in the same recipe, one selected for its pungency, perhaps; another to add a hint of sweetness.

For years, the only chillies in our markets and supermarkets were the slim tapered red and green serranos or cayennes. However, travellers titillated by the tastes of spicy dishes in other countries have prompted a demand for a wider range of chillies. We can now look forward to getting to know this exciting ingredient better, not only in its fresh form, but also dried, and in sauces, salsas and pickles. Take the chilli challenge – and add an exciting twist to your cooking.

Jenny Fleetwood

Types of Chilli

ANAHEIM

These large Mexican chillies are mild to medium hot. They can be stuffed or used in sauces, stews and salsas.

JALAPENO

Available green or red, fresh or pickled, jalapeños are hot and are used in tamales, salsas and sauces.

HABANERO

Also known as Scotch Bonnet, these chillies are extremely hot. They are used in Caribbean jerk sauces.

THAI

These tiny chillies are fairly hot and are used in Thai curry paste and salads.

ANCHO

These are dried and are mild and quite sweet.

CASCABEL

Round, dried cascabel chillies rattle when shaken.

CHIPOTLE

The dried, smoked versions of jalapeño chillies, chipotle chillies give an intense heat to soups or stews.

GUAJILLO

Fairly mild in flavour, and very good with seafood.

TEPIN

Tiny and blisteringly hot, tepin chillies are used to make hot pepper sauce for Thai cuisine.

INDIAN

Small and very hot, these are used in curries.

CAYENNE, HOT CHILLI POWDER AND CHILLI FLAKES

Cayenne is a pungent spice made from blended red chillies, chilli powder can be ground chillies or a special mix, and chilli flakes are crushed dried chillies. All are used to spice up sausages, sauces and oils.

MINCED CHILLI, CHILLI OIL AND HOT RED PEPPER SAUCE

Minced chilli is a paste made from ground red chillies. Chilli oil is good for frying, or basting meat or fish on the barbecue. Hot red pepper sauce is very popular in Malaysian and Caribbean cuisine.

Jalapeño

Cayenne

Hot chilli powder

Chilli flakes

Ancho

Habanero

Indian

Anaheim

Thai

Cascabel

Tepin

Guajillo

Minced chilli

Chilli oil

Hot red pepper sauce

Chipotle

$\mathcal{B}$ASIC $\mathcal{T}$ECHNIQUES

PREPARING CHILLIES

The oil in chillies contains a chemical, capsaicin, which is a strong irritant, so it is vital to handle chillies with care. Work in a well-ventilated area and wear gloves, if possible. To prepare, slit chillies lengthways with a sharp knife. Scrape out the seeds.

Slice the chillies or chop them finely. Much of the heat is concentrated in the seeds, so you may prefer to discard some or all of them. If you have worked without gloves, wash your hands several times in soapy water. Avoid touching your face, especially the eye area.

"FIRE" EXTINGUISHERS

If you have managed to get chilli oil on delicate skin, an alkali such as a paste made from bicarbonate of soda and water will help to ease the discomfort. Equally, if you inadvertently chomp on a chilli and feel as though your mouth is on fire, reach for bread, rice, natural yogurt or milk. Whatever you do, avoid sparkling water or any other fizzy drink, or your tongue will feel as if someone is using it for target practice.

CHOOSING CHILLIES

- Fresh chillies should be firm, glossy and evenly coloured. Avoid musty or soft chillies.
- If fresh chillies are not available, use canned ones, but taste a tiny portion to judge the heat and therefore the quantity required.
- It is a good idea to buy dried chillies in transparent packaging, so that you can see the quality at a glance.

- If dried chillies look a little dusty when you remove them from the packaging, don't worry. Just wipe them gently with a piece of kitchen paper before use.
- Chilli flakes and ground chillies should have good aroma and colour. If chilli powder looks dark, this is not a sign that it is stale, rather an indication that the chillies have been mixed with other spices, American-style.

STORING CHILLIES

• The best way to store fresh chillies is to wrap them well in kitchen paper, place them in a plastic bag, and keep them in the chiller compartment of your fridge. They will keep well for a week or more, but it is a good idea to check them occasionally and discard any that begin to show signs of softening.

• Chillies can also be frozen. There is no need to blanch them if you plan to use them fairly quickly.

• Store ground chillies in airtight jars in a cool place out of direct sunlight. Buy small quantities and use as soon as possible. Some cooks store dried chillies (and curry powder) in the freezer.

• To dry your own fresh chillies, thread them on a string, hang them in a warm, dry place until they are crumbly, then use a pestle to crush them in a mortar.

• Pack chillies in a sterilized jar and pour over sherry to cover. Close tightly and store in a cool, dark place. You can use both the chillies and the sherry for flavouring.

MAKING A CHILLI FLOWER

Chilli flowers make a very pretty garnish. Carefully slit each chilli lengthways and scrape out the seeds, taking care not to damage the flesh. Keeping the chilli intact at the stem end, cut it into as many fine strips as possible.

Drop the chillies into a bowl of iced water, cover and chill for several hours. The iced water will make the chilli strips curl back. Drain well on kitchen paper and garnish the food with the chillies just before serving. Chilli flowers are not edible.

CHILLI RELISH

Make this at least 1 hour before serving to allow the flavours to blend. Chop 2 large tomatoes finely. Place them in a mixing bowl.

Chop 1 red onion and 1 garlic clove. Add to the tomatoes, mix well, then stir in 10ml/2 tsp chilli sauce (use a sweet chilli sauce or a hot one, as you like).

Stir in 15ml/1 tbsp chopped fresh basil and 1 chopped green chilli – with the seeds if you like a hot relish – then add a pinch each of salt and sugar.

COOK'S TIPS

• Unless chillies are very thin-skinned, they will benefit from being peeled. Char them under a hot grill, or by turning them in a gas flame. Put the hot chillies in a bowl, cover with several layers of kitchen paper and leave for 10 minutes. Rub off the skin with gloved fingers or scrape with a sharp knife.

• To reduce the heat of fresh or dried chillies, soak them for an hour in a solution of wine vinegar and salt in the ratio 3:1.

• To bring out the flavour of chillies, dry roast them in a hot non-stick frying pan for a few minutes. Do not let them change colour.

• Chilli and cheese make perfect partners. Stir about 5ml/1 tsp sweet chilli sauce (or a seeded roasted chilli) into 115g/4oz/1 cup grated mature Cheddar cheese, then beat in an egg. Toast bread on one side only, pile the cheese mixture on the untoasted side and grill until puffy and golden.

HARISSA

For a delicious taste, brush a small amount of this fiery North African sauce over chicken wings before grilling them. In its country of origin, harissa is used as a condiment with meat or rice dishes.

Remove the seeds from 115g/4oz dried red chillies, then soak them in warm water to cover until soft. Drain well. Using scissors, snip the chillies into chunks, then pound them to a paste in a pestle and mortar. Add 4 chopped garlic cloves, 2.5ml/½ tsp salt, 15ml/1 tbsp ground cumin and 10ml/2 tsp each of dried mint and caraway seeds. Grind to a paste, then stir in 60ml/4 tbsp olive oil. Scrape into a sterilized jar, cover with a layer of olive oil and chill. It can be kept in the fridge for up to 6 weeks.

PICKLED CHILLIES

Here are two excellent ways of dealing with a glut of fresh chillies. The easiest way to pickle chillies is to slit them, remove the seeds and pack them in sterilized jars with spiced vinegar to cover. Alternatively, cut off the tops, leaving the cores and seeds intact, then slice the chillies in half widthways. Blanch them in a 50:50 mixture of white vinegar and water, with a little salt. Leave it to cool, then pack into sterilized jars, tucking whole peeled garlic cloves between the layers. Fill the jars with olive oil, close tightly and leave for at least 2 weeks before using.

ROUILLE   *Traditionally added to bouillabaisse, this is a French red chilli mayonnaise.*

Peel and seed 1 fresh red chilli, then pound it to a paste with 2 garlic cloves. Scrape the mixture into a bowl and add 2 egg yolks, a pinch of salt and pepper, 5ml/1 tsp red pepper mustard and 15ml/1 tbsp lemon juice. Whisk in 1.5ml/¼ tsp cayenne pepper. Have ready 250ml/8fl oz/1 cup of equal quantities of olive oil and sunflower oil. Whisking constantly, add the oil to the mixture, drop by drop, then in a slow stream, until the mixture thickens. Makes 300ml/½ pint/1¼ cups

Scintillating Soups, Starters and Snacks

Chillies stimulate the appetite, so what better way to start a meal than with one of these delicious dishes? Many of them double as tasty snacks to liven up a drinks party.

PRAWN, MINT AND CHILLI SALAD

Coconut milk and lime juice tame the fiery taste of chillies in this superb salad.

Serves 4

12 large prawns, thawed if frozen

15ml/1 tbsp butter

15ml/1 tbsp fish sauce

juice of 1 lime

45ml/3 tbsp thin coconut milk

5ml/1 tsp caster sugar

1 garlic clove, crushed

2.5cm/1in piece of fresh root ginger,
*   peeled and grated*

2 fresh red chillies, seeded and
*   finely chopped*

30ml/2 tbsp fresh mint leaves

ground black pepper

coconut strips, to garnish

225g/8oz lettuce leaves, to serve

COOK'S TIP

This makes a warm salad, but the prawns will have a better flavour if left to marinate in the sauce for 1 hour.

Peel the prawns, leaving the tails intact. Slit the back of each prawn, working from the tail to the head, and remove the black vein.

Melt the butter in a large frying pan and add the prawns. Toss them over the heat until they turn pink.

Mix the fish sauce, lime juice, coconut milk, sugar, garlic, ginger and chillies in a bowl. Add black pepper to taste. Add the warm prawns to the sauce with the mint leaves. Toss and leave to marinate. Serve the prawn mixture on a bed of lettuce leaves garnished with coconut strips.

TORTILLA AND CHILLI SOUP

This tasty soup, with fresh green chillies and tortillas, has more than a hint of Mexican flavour.

Serves 4

1 onion, finely chopped

1 garlic clove, crushed

15ml/1 tbsp vegetable oil

2 tomatoes, peeled, seeded
   and chopped

2.5ml/½ tsp salt

2.4 litres/4 pints/10 cups
   chicken stock

1 carrot, diced

1 small courgette, diced

1 boneless chicken breast, cooked,
   skinned and finely sliced

2 green chillies, seeded and chopped

For the garnish

4 corn tortillas

oil for frying

1 ripe avocado, peeled, stoned
   and diced

2 spring onions, chopped

30ml/2tbsp chopped fresh coriander

Fry the onion and garlic in the oil for 5-8 minutes. Add the tomatoes and salt and cook for 5 minutes. Add the stock, bring to the boil, then simmer, covered, for about 15 minutes. Meanwhile, for the garnish, cut the tortillas into strips. Pour about 1cm/½in of oil into a frying pan and heat until the oil is hot. Add the tortilla strips in batches and fry until they just begin to brown. Remove with a slotted spoon and drain on kitchen paper. Add the carrot to the soup and cook, covered, for 10 minutes. Add the courgette, chicken and chillies and cook, uncovered, for 5 minutes. Divide the tortilla strips and avocado among four soup bowls. Ladle in the soup, then scatter the spring onions and coriander on top. Serve immediately.

BEEF CHILLI SOUP

Based on a traditional recipe, this hearty soup with fresh red chillies makes a warming start to any meal.
Serve it with plenty of crusty bread.

Serves 4

15ml/1 tbsp vegetable oil

1 onion, chopped

175g/6oz minced beef

2 garlic cloves, chopped

1 fresh red chilli, sliced

60ml/4 tbsp plain flour

400g/14oz can chopped tomatoes

600ml/1 pint/2½ cups beef stock

225/8oz/1¾ cups drained, canned
  kidney beans

salt and ground black pepper

30ml/2 tbsp chopped fresh parsley,
  to garnish

crusty bread, to serve

COOK'S TIP
For a milder flavour, remove
the seeds from the chilli after
you have sliced it.

Heat the oil in a large saucepan. Add the onion and minced beef and fry for 5 minutes until brown and sealed. Stir the mixture frequently.

Stir in the garlic, chilli and flour. Cook for 1 minute. Add the tomatoes and pour in the stock. Bring to the boil, stirring all the time.

Stir in the kidney beans and season with plenty of salt and pepper. Cook for a further 20 minutes.

Check the seasoning, then pour into heated soup bowls. Sprinkle with fresh parsley and serve at once with crusty bread.

STEAMED CHILLI MUSSELS

This is a glorious treat for all lovers of spicy seafood. If you are one of those who like your food hot, simply add more fresh chillies to taste.

Serves 6

2 fresh chillies

6 ripe tomatoes

30ml/2 tbsp peanut oil

2 garlic cloves, crushed

2 shallots, finely chopped

1kg/2¼lb fresh mussels, scrubbed
   and beards removed

30ml/2 tbsp white wine

30ml/2 tbsp chopped fresh parsley,
   to garnish

French bread, to serve (optional)

COOK'S TIP

When preparing the mussels, discard any that are not tightly closed, or which do not snap shut if you tap them sharply. The opposite rule applies to the cooked mussels. Discard any that fail to open.

Chop the fresh chillies roughly and remove the seeds. Chop the tomatoes into small pieces.

Heat the peanut oil in a large, heavy-based saucepan and gently sauté the garlic and shallots until soft. Stir in the tomatoes and chilli and simmer for 10 minutes.

Add the prepared mussels and white wine to the saucepan, cover tightly and cook, shaking the pan frequently, for about 5 minutes, or until all the mussel shells have opened. Scatter over the chopped parsley. Serve in a large bowl with chunks of fresh French bread, if liked.

GARLIC CHILLI PRAWNS

Served piping hot and sizzling with flavour, these Spanish-style prawns are stir-fried in olive oil spiced with fresh red chilli and garlic to make a delicious starter.

Serves 4

60ml/4 tbsp olive oil

2-3 garlic cloves, finely chopped

1 fresh red chilli, seeded and chopped

16 cooked Mediterranean prawns

15ml/1 tbsp chopped fresh parsley

salt and ground black pepper

lemon wedges and flat leaf parsley,
   to garnish

French bread, to serve (optional)

COOK'S TIP

Add a dash or two of Tabasco just before serving the prawns, if you like.

Heat the oil in a large frying pan and add the garlic and chilli. Stir-fry for 1 minute, until the garlic begins to turn brown.

Add the Mediterranean prawns and stir-fry for 3–4 minutes, coating them well with the flavoured oil. Add salt and pepper to taste.

Sprinkle in the parsley, remove from the heat and place the prawns into a heated serving bowl. Pour the flavoured oil over. Serve with French bread to mop up the juices, if liked. Garnish the prawns with lemon wedges and flat leaf parsley.

DEEP-FRIED WONTONS WITH CHILLI SAMBAL

The sambal, a spicy sauce made with fresh red chillies, makes a hot and fiery dip for these delicious crisp appetizers. You can prepare the wontons in advance and freeze them.

Makes 40

115g/4oz pork fillet, trimmed
  and sliced
225g/8oz cooked prawns, peeled
  and de-veined
2-3 garlic cloves, crushed
2 spring onions, roughly chopped
15ml/1 tbsp cornflour
about 40 wonton wrappers
oil, for deep-frying
salt and ground black pepper

For the chilli sambal

1-2 fresh red chillies, seeded
  and sliced
1-2 garlic cloves, crushed
45ml/3 tbsp dark soy sauce
45-60ml/3-4 tbsp lemon or lime juice

Grind the slices of pork finely in a food processor or blender. Add the prawns, garlic, spring onions and cornflour. Season to taste and then process briefly.

Position the wonton wrapper like a diamond in front of you. Place a little of the prepared filling on to each wrapper, just off centre. Dampen all the edges with water, except for the uppermost corner of the diamond.

Lift the corner nearest to you towards the filling and then roll up the wrapper once, to cover the filling. Turn over. Bring the two extreme corners together, sealing one on top of the other. Squeeze lightly, to plump up the filling. Repeat until all the wrappers and the filling have been used up. Set the filled wontons aside.

Prepare the sambal. Mix the chillies and garlic together in a bowl, then stir in the dark soy sauce and the lemon or lime juice. Add enough water (15-30ml/1-2 tbsp) to make a dipping sauce. Pour the sambal into a small serving bowl and set aside.

Heat the oil in a deep-fryer to 190°C/375°F, or until a cube of day-old bread browns in 30 seconds. Deep-fry the filled wontons in batches for about 2–3 minutes, or until cooked through, crisp and golden brown. Remove with a slotted spoon and drain on kitchen paper. If frozen, they will need about 4 minutes. Serve on a large platter, with the chilli sambal.

TORTILLA TURNOVERS WITH CHEESE AND CHILLI FILLING

These delicious fried turnovers, spiced with jalapeño chillies, come from Mexico, where they are called Quesadillas. *This size makes a popular snack and smaller versions can be served as canapés.*

Makes 14

14 freshly prepared unbaked tortillas

For the filling

225g/8oz/2 cups finely chopped or
grated Cheddar cheese
3 fresh jalapeño chillies, seeded and
cut into strips
oil, for shallow frying
salt
shredded lettuce, to serve

COOK'S TIP

For other stuffing ideas, try
leftover beans with chillies, or
chopped chorizo sausage, fried
with a little chopped onion.

Combine the cheese and chilli in a bowl. Season with salt and set aside. Heat the oil in a frying pan. Hold an unbaked tortilla in the palm of your hand and put a spoonful of filling along the centre, avoiding the edges.

Fold the tortilla and seal the edges by pressing or crimping well together. Put it in the hot oil. Repeat with two more tortillas, or as many as the frying pan will hold. Fry each batch until golden brown and crisp on both sides.

Using a fish slice, lift out the turnovers and drain them on kitchen paper. Transfer to a plate and keep hot. Serve at once on a bed of lettuce.

NACHOS WITH CHILLI BEEF

Nachos spiced up with a red chilli and minced beef topping make an irresistible starter or snack.

Serves 4

225g/8oz minced beef

2 fresh red chillies, sliced

3 spring onions, chopped

175g/6oz nachos

300ml/½ pint/1¼ cups soured cream

50g/2oz/½ cup grated
   Cheddar cheese

salt and ground black pepper

Dry-fry the minced beef and chillies in a large frying pan for 10 minutes, stirring all the time, then add the spring onions and cook for 5 minutes more. Stir in salt and pepper to taste. Preheat the grill.

Arrange the nachos in four individual flameproof dishes. Spoon on the minced beef mixture, then top with the soured cream and grated cheese. Grill under a medium heat for 5 minutes. Serve at once.

COOK'S TIP
Use finely chopped gherkins instead of spring onions, and Red Leicester instead of Cheddar cheese, if you like.

CORN FRITTERS WITH CHILLI SALSA

The chilli salsa adds piquancy to the lightly spiced fritters.

Makes about 48

corn or other vegetable oil

450g/1lb/3 cups canned sweetcorn

115g/4oz/1 cup plain flour

50g/2oz/½ cup cornmeal

250ml/8fl oz/1 cup milk

10ml/2 tsp baking powder

10ml/2 tsp sugar

5ml/1 tsp salt

2.5ml/½ tsp grated nutmeg

2.5ml/½ tsp cayenne pepper

4 eggs, lightly beaten

lettuce, cherry tomatoes and fresh coriander, to serve

For the salsa

115g/4oz cherry tomatoes, chopped

115g/4oz/¾ cup canned sweetcorn

1 red pepper, finely chopped

½ small red onion, finely chopped

juice of 1 lemon

30ml/2 tbsp olive oil

30ml/2 tbsp chopped fresh coriander

1-2 fresh chillies, seeded and finely chopped

Prepare the salsa at least 2 hours ahead. Drain the sweetcorn then combine all the ingredients in a medium-size bowl, crushing them lightly with the back of a spoon to release the juices. Cover and refrigerate until ready to use.

Put 30ml/2 tbsp of the oil in a medium-size bowl. Add the sweetcorn (drained), flour, cornmeal, milk, baking powder, sugar, salt, nutmeg, cayenne and eggs. Mix until just blended; do not overbeat. If the batter is too stiff, stir in a little more milk or water. Unless you plan to serve the fritters as soon as they are cooked, preheat the oven to 160°C/325°F/Gas 3.

Heat oil to a depth of 1cm/½in in a large heavy-based frying pan until hot but not smoking. Drop tablespoons of batter into the hot oil, a few at a time, and cook for 3–4 minutes until golden, turning once. Remove with a slotted spoon and drain on kitchen paper. Arrange the corn fritters on a serving plate and top each one with a spoonful of salsa. Serve at once with lettuce, tomatoes and coriander. Alternatively, arrange the fritters on baking sheets and keep them warm for up to 1 hour in the oven.

MEXICAN DIP WITH CHILLI CHIPS

Fresh red chilli gives a hint of heat to the avocado dip and the chips are fired up with chilli powder.

Serves 4

2 ripe avocados

juice of 1 lime

½ small onion, finely chopped

½ fresh red chilli, seeded and
   finely chopped

3 tomatoes, peeled, seeded
   and chopped

30ml/2 tbsp chopped fresh coriander

30ml/2 tbsp soured cream

salt and ground black pepper

15ml/1 tbsp soured cream and
   a pinch of cayenne pepper,
   to garnish

For the chips

150g/5oz tortilla chips

30ml/2 tbsp finely grated mature
   Cheddar cheese

1.5ml/¼ tsp chilli powder

30ml/2 tbsp chopped fresh parsley

Cut the avocados in half, lift out the stones and scoop out the flesh with a spoon, scraping the shells well.

Place the flesh in a blender or food processor. Add the lime juice, chopped onion, chilli, tomatoes, chopped coriander and soured cream, with salt to taste and a generous grinding of black pepper. Process until fairly smooth. Scrape into a bowl, cover tightly and place in the fridge till needed.

Meanwhile, preheat the grill, then scatter the tortilla chips over a baking sheet. Mix the grated Cheddar cheese with the chilli powder, sprinkle over the chips and grill for 1–2 minutes, until the cheese has melted. Sprinkle with the parsley.

Remove the avocado dip from the fridge, top with the soured cream and sprinkle with cayenne pepper. Serve the bowl on a large plate surrounded by the chilli tortilla chips.

Fiery Main Meals

Many of the world's finest chilli dishes come from India and Thailand: some fast and fiery; others spicy and subtle. Here are some favourites, with contributions from other countries too.

SALMON WITH SPICY CHILLI PESTO

The pesto is unusual because it uses sunflower kernels and fresh red chillies as its flavouring rather than the classic basil and pine nuts.

Serves 4

4 salmon steaks, about
   225g/8oz each
30ml/2 tbsp sunflower oil
finely grated rind and juice of 1 lime
lime wedges, to serve

For the spicy chilli pesto

6 mild fresh red chillies, seeded
2 garlic cloves
30ml/2 tbsp pumpkin seeds or
   sunflower seeds
finely grated rind and juice of 1 lime
75ml/5 tbsp olive oil
salt and ground black pepper

COOK'S TIP
*For a fast supper, you can pay
a little more and buy salmon
fillet. If you do have time, try
this method of boning steaks.*

Insert a sharp knife close to the top of the bone of a salmon steak. Working close to the bone, cut your way to the end of the steak until one side of the steak has been released and one side is still attached. Repeat with the other side. Pull out any visible bones with a pair of tweezers. Cut away the skin in one piece. Form each piece of fish into a circle, with the thinner end wrapped around the fatter end. Secure tightly with a length of string.

Rub oil into the fish. Add the lime rind and juice and chill for 2 hours.

To make the pesto, process the chillies, garlic, seeds, lime rind, lime juice and seasoning in a food processor or blender until well mixed. With the motor running, gradually add the oil through the feeder tube until the sauce has thickened and emulsified. Preheat the grill. Drain the salmon and grill for 5 minutes each side. Serve with the pesto and lime wedges.

STEAMED FISH WITH CHILLI SAUCE

This sweet chilli sauce is delicious, but can come as a bit of a shock to the uninitiated. If you are unaccustomed to fiery flavours, reduce the number of red chillies.

Serves 4

1 large fish, or 2 medium firm fish,
    such as bass or grouper, scaled
    and cleaned

1 fresh banana leaf

30ml/2 tbsp rice wine

3 fresh red chillies, seeded and
    finely sliced

2 garlic cloves, finely chopped

2cm/¾in piece of fresh root ginger,
    finely shredded

2 lemon grass stalks, crushed and
    finely chopped

2 spring onions, chopped

30ml/2 tbsp fish sauce

juice of 1 lime

For the chilli sauce

10 red chillies, seeded and chopped

4 garlic cloves, chopped

60ml/4 tbsp fish sauce

15ml/1 tbsp sugar

75ml/5 tbsp lime juice

Rinse the fish inside and out under cold running water. Pat dry with kitchen paper. With a sharp knife, slash the skin of the fish a few times on both sides.

Place the fish on the banana leaf. Mix together all the remaining ingredients and spread over the fish.

Place a small upturned plate in the bottom of a wok and pour in boiling water to a depth of 5cm/2in. Lift the banana leaf, with the fish, and support it on the plate in the wok. Cover with a lid. Steam for 10–15 minutes, or until the fish is cooked.

Meanwhile, place all the ingredients for the chilli sauce in a food processor or blender and process until smooth. You may need to add a little cold water.

Serve the fish hot, on the banana leaf if you like, with the sweet chilli sauce in a bowl to spoon over the top.

MONKFISH WITH GREEN CHILLI SALSA

Marinated monkfish is doubly delicious served Mexican-style, with a spicy green chilli salsa.

Serves 4

675g/1½lb monkfish tail
45ml/3 tbsp olive oil
30ml/2 tbsp lime juice
1 garlic clove, crushed
15ml/1 tbsp chopped fresh coriander
salt and ground black pepper
coriander sprigs and lime slices,
   to garnish

For the green chilli salsa

4 tomatoes
1 avocado
½ red onion, chopped
1 green chilli, seeded and chopped
30ml/2 tbsp chopped fresh coriander
30ml/2 tbsp olive oil
15ml/1 tbsp lime juice

To make the salsa, cut a cross in the top of each of the tomatoes. Dip them in boiling water for 30 seconds, then drain, peel off the skins and dice the flesh. Cut the avocado in half, lift out the stone and remove the peel. Dice the avocado flesh. Mix the tomatoes, avocado, onion, chilli, coriander, olive oil and lime juice in a bowl. Cover and leave at room temperature for about 40 minutes.

Meanwhile, prepare the monkfish. Using a sharp knife, remove the pinkish-grey membrane. Cut the fillets from either side of the backbone, then cut each fillet in half to give four steaks.

Mix the oil, lime juice, garlic and coriander in a shallow non-metallic dish. Add a little salt and pepper, then lay the monkfish steaks in the dish. Turn them several times to coat with the marinade, then cover the dish and marinate the fish at a cool room temperature or in the fridge for 30 minutes. Preheat the grill.

Drain the monkfish, reserving the marinade. Grill for 10–12 minutes, turning once and brushing regularly with the marinade, until the steaks are cooked through.

Serve the monkfish garnished with coriander sprigs and lime slices and accompanied by the green chilli salsa.

CHICKEN WITH CHILLIES AND CASHEW NUTS

Chicken with red chillies cashew nuts and a touch of garlic make this a delicious stir-fry.

Serves 4–6

450g/1lb chicken breasts, boned and skinned

30ml/2 tbsp vegetable oil

2 garlic cloves, sliced

4 dried red chillies, chopped

1 red pepper, seeded and cut into 2cm/³⁄₄in dice

30ml/2 tbsp oyster sauce

15ml/1 tbsp soy sauce

pinch of granulated sugar

1 bunch of spring onions, cut into 5cm/2in lengths

175g/6oz/1¹⁄₂ cups cashew nuts, roasted

fresh coriander leaves, to garnish

With a sharp knife, cut the chicken into bite-size pieces. Heat a wok, add the oil and swirl it around gently. Add the garlic and dried chillies and fry until the garlic is golden.

Add the chicken and stir-fry until it changes colour, then add the red pepper. If necessary, moisten with a little water.

Stir in the oyster sauce, soy sauce and sugar. Add the spring onions and cashew nuts. Stir–fry for 1–2 minutes more. Serve, garnished with fresh coriander leaves.

CHICKEN IN ALMOND AND CHILLI SAUCE

Green pepper and jalapeño chilli combine with tomatillos to make this popular Mexican dish.

Serves 6

1.5kg/3-3½lb chicken, cut into
   serving pieces
475ml/16fl oz/2 cups chicken stock
1 onion, chopped
1 garlic clove, chopped
115g/4oz/2 cups fresh coriander,
   roughly chopped
1 green pepper, seeded and chopped
1 jalapeño chilli, seeded and chopped
275g/10oz can tomatillos (Mexican
   green tomatoes)
115g/4oz/1 cup ground almonds
30ml/2 tbsp corn oil
salt
fresh coriander sprig, to garnish
rice, to serve

Put the chicken pieces into a shallow pan with the stock. Bring to a simmer, cover and cook for about 45 minutes, until tender. Drain the stock into a measuring jug and set aside.

Put the onion, garlic, coriander, pepper, chilli, tomatillos with their juice and the almonds in a food processor or blender. Purée fairly coarsely.

Heat the oil in a frying pan, add the almond mixture and cook over a low heat, stirring for 3–4 minutes. Scrape into the pan with the chicken.

Make the stock up to 475ml/16fl oz/2 cups with water, if necessary. Stir it into the pan. Mix gently and simmer for just long enough to blend the flavours and heat the chicken pieces through. Add salt to taste. Serve at once, garnished with coriander and accompanied by rice.

COCONUT CHICKEN WITH GREEN CHILLI PASTE

This green curry, from Thailand, owes its delicious spicy flavour to fresh green chillies.

Serves 4–6

1.2kg/2½lb chicken, without giblets
600ml/1 pint/2½ cups coconut milk
450ml/¾ pint/1¾ cups chicken stock
2 lime leaves
10ml/2 tsp coriander seeds
2.5ml/½ tsp cumin seeds
4 fresh green chillies, finely chopped
20ml/4 tsp sugar
10ml/2 tsp salt
7.5cm/3in piece of lemon grass
30ml/2 tbsp chopped fresh root ginger
3 garlic cloves, crushed
1 onion, finely chopped
2cm/¾in piece dried shrimp paste
45ml/3 tbsp each chopped coriander
* leaves and chopped fresh mint*
2.5ml/½ tsp ground nutmeg
30ml/2 tbsp vegetable oil
1 sweet potato, peeled and diced
1 small butternut squash, peeled,
* seeded and roughly chopped*
115g/4oz French beans
fresh coriander, to garnish

Cut the chicken into serving pieces. Remove the skin. Strain the coconut milk into a bowl, reserving the solids in the strainer. Place the chicken in a pan, cover with the thin coconut milk and the stock. Add the lime leaves and simmer, uncovered, for 40 minutes. Lift out the chicken, take it off the bone and set it aside.

To make the paste, dry-fry the seeds in a wok. Using a mortar and pestle, grind the chillies with the sugar and salt to make a smooth paste. Add the seeds from the wok, lemon grass, ginger, garlic and onion, then grind smoothly. Add the shrimp paste, herbs, nutmeg and oil and mix well.

Place a ladleful of the chicken cooking liquid in a large wok. Add 60-75ml/4-5 tbsp of the curry paste to the liquid, according to taste. Mix well. Boil rapidly until the liquid has reduced completely. Add the remaining cooking liquid with the chicken, sweet potato, squash and beans (trimmed and halved). Simmer for 10–15 minutes until the sweet potato is cooked. Just before serving, stir in the thick part of the coconut milk and simmer gently to thicken. Serve garnished with shredded coriander.

CHILLI PORK RIBS WITH GREEN BEANS

A pungent chilli paste made from dried red chillies gives this stir-fry an unforgettable flavour.

Serves 4–6

675g/1½lb pork spare ribs (or belly of pork)

30ml/2 tbsp vegetable oil

15ml/1 tbsp palm sugar

15ml/1 tbsp fish sauce

150g/5oz/1 cup fine green beans, trimmed and cut into 5cm/2in lengths

2 kaffir lime leaves, finely sliced

2 fresh red chillies, finely sliced, to garnish

For the chilli paste

3 dried red chillies, seeded and soaked

4 shallots, chopped

4 garlic cloves, chopped

5ml/1 tsp chopped galangal or fresh root ginger

1 lemon grass stalk, chopped

6 black peppercorns

5ml/1 tsp shrimp paste

30ml/2 tbsp dried shrimp, rinsed

Put all the ingredients for the chilli paste in a mortar and grind with a pestle until the mixture forms a thick paste.

Slice and chop the spare ribs or belly pork into 4cm/1½in lengths.

Heat the oil in a wok or large frying pan. Add the pork and fry for about 5 minutes, until lightly browned.

Stir in the chilli paste and continue to cook for another 5 minutes, stirring constantly to stop the paste from sticking to the pan.

Pour in 120ml/4fl oz/½ cup water, cover and simmer for 7–10 minutes or until the spare ribs are tender. Stir in the palm sugar and fish sauce and taste to check the seasoning.

Add the green beans and kaffir lime leaves and fry until the beans are cooked. Serve garnished with sliced red chillies.

STIR-FRIED BEEF IN OYSTER AND CHILLI SAUCE

Red chillies add tongue-tingling heat to this tasty beef stir-fry.

Serves 4–6

450g/1lb rump steak

30ml/2 tbsp soy sauce

15ml/1 tbsp cornflour

45ml/3 tbsp vegetable oil

15ml/1 tbsp chopped garlic

15ml/1 tbsp chopped fresh root ginger

225g/8oz/2 cups mixed mushrooms
   such as shiitake, oyster and straw

15ml/1 tbsp oyster sauce

15ml/1 tbsp sweet chilli sauce

5ml/1 tsp granulated sugar

ground black pepper

4 spring onions, cut into short lengths

2 red chillies, seeded and cut
   into strips

COOK'S TIP

Made from extracts of oysters, oyster sauce is smooth with a savoury-sweet and meaty taste.

Slice the beef on the diagonal into long thin strips. Mix the soy sauce and cornflour in a large bowl, stir in the beef, cover and leave to marinate for 1–2 hours.

Heat half the oil in a wok or large frying pan. Add the garlic and ginger and fry until fragrant. Stir in the beef. Stir to separate the strips, let them colour, then cook for 1–2 minutes. Remove from the wok and set aside.

Heat the remaining oil in the wok. Add the shiitake, oyster and straw mushrooms. Stir-fry until tender.

Return the beef to the wok and mix it with the mushrooms. Add the oyster sauce, chilli sauce and sugar, with black pepper to taste. Mix well, then add the spring onions and red chillies. Stir to mix. Serve at once.

MADRAS CURRY

Fresh green and red chillies add bite to this medium-hot curry.

Serves 4–6

60ml/4 tbsp vegetable oil

1 large onion, finely sliced

3-4 cloves

4 green cardamoms, bruised

2 whole star anise

4 fresh green chillies, chopped

2 fresh red chillies, chopped

45ml/3 tbsp Madras curry paste

5ml/1 tsp ground turmeric

450g/1lb lean beef, cubed

60ml/4 tbsp tamarind juice

salt and sugar, to taste

fresh coriander sprig, to garnish

COOK'S TIP

If the curry is a little too hot for your taste, just spoon a dollop of natural yogurt or raita (yogurt and cucumber sambal) on the top.

Heat the oil in a flameproof casserole and fry the onion until golden brown. Lower the heat, add the cloves, cardamoms, star anise, chillies, curry paste and turmeric. Mix well. Fry for another 2–3 minutes.

Add the beef and mix well to coat it in the spices. Cover and cook on a low heat for 1 hour, or until the beef is tender, stirring occasionally. Increase the heat and cook, uncovered, for a few minutes more to reduce any excess cooking liquid.

Stir in the tamarind juice, with salt and sugar to taste. Reheat the dish and serve hot, garnished with the fresh coriander.

PORK CHOPS WITH SOUR GREEN CHILLI SALSA

Roasted chillies are the secret of this salsa's success. It is particularly good with pork but could also be served with chicken or prawns.

Serves 4

30ml/2 tbsp vegetable oil

15ml/1 tbsp fresh lemon juice

10ml/2 tsp ground cumin

5ml/1 tsp dried oregano

8 pork loin chops, about
*   2cm/¾in thick*

salt and ground black pepper

lettuce, chopped tomatoes and pepper,
*   to serve*

For the salsa

2 fresh hot green chillies

2 green peppers, seeded and chopped

1 tomato, peeled and seeded

½ onion, roughly chopped

4 spring onions

1 drained pickled jalapeño chilli,
*   stem removed*

30ml/2 tbsp olive oil

30ml/2 tbsp fresh lime juice

45ml/3 tbsp cider vinegar

5ml/1 tsp salt

Combine the vegetable oil, lemon juice, cumin and oregano in a small bowl. Add pepper to taste and stir to mix.

Arrange the pork chops in one layer in a shallow dish, brushing each chop with the oil mixture on both sides. Cover and leave to stand for 2–3 hours at a cool room temperature, or overnight in the fridge.

To make the salsa, roast the chillies over a gas flame, holding them with tongs, until charred on all sides. (Alternatively, char the skins under the grill.) Leave to cool for 5 minutes. Wearing rubber gloves, remove the charred skin. For a less fiery flavour, discard the seeds.

Place the chillies in a food processor or blender. Add the remaining salsa ingredients. Process until finely chopped; do not purée.

Transfer the salsa to a heavy-based saucepan and simmer for about 15 minutes, stirring occasionally. Set aside.

Season the pork chops. Heat a ridged pan. (Alternatively, preheat the grill.) When hot, add the pork chops and cook for about 5 minutes, until browned. Turn and continue cooking for 5–7 minutes more or until cooked through. Work in batches, if necessary. Serve at once, with the sour green chilli salsa, lettuce, chopped tomatoes and pepper.

CHILLI, TOMATO AND SPINACH PIZZA

This richly flavoured topping with fresh chillies makes a tasty and satisfying pizza.

Serves 3

*45ml/3 tbsp tomato oil (from jar of
   sun-dried tomatoes)*

1 onion, chopped

2 garlic cloves, chopped

*1-2 fresh chillies, seeded and
   finely chopped*

*4 drained sun-dried tomatoes in oil,
   roughly chopped*

400g/14oz can chopped tomatoes

15ml/1 tbsp tomato purée

175g/6oz fresh spinach

1 pizza base, 25-30cm/10-12in

*75g/3oz smoked Bavarian
   cheese, grated*

*75g/3oz/3/4 cup grated mature
   Cheddar cheese*

salt and ground black pepper

COOK'S TIP
*Use sun-dried tomato paste for
extra flavour, if you like.*

Heat 30ml/2 tbsp of the tomato oil, add the onion, garlic and chillies and fry gently for about 5 minutes until soft. Add the sun-dried tomatoes, chopped tomatoes and tomato purée to the pan and season to taste. Bring to the boil, then simmer uncovered, stirring occasionally for 15 minutes.

Remove the stalks from the spinach, rinse the leaves and pat dry with kitchen paper. Chop the spinach and stir it into the sauce. Cook, stirring, for 5–10 minutes, until the spinach has wilted and no excess moisture remains. Leave to cool. Preheat the oven to 220°C/425°F/Gas 7.

Brush the pizza base with the remaining oil, then spoon over the sauce. Scatter over the cheeses and bake for 15–20 minutes until crisp and golden.

CHILLI CON CARNE

An all-time favourite, this hot and spicy dish uses both fresh chillies and chilli powder.

Serves 8

45ml/3 tbsp vegetable oil

1 large onion, chopped

2 fresh red chillies, seeded and sliced

900g/2lb minced beef

4 garlic cloves, crushed

15ml/1 tbsp soft light brown sugar

30–45ml/2-3 tbsp chilli powder

5ml/1 tsp ground cumin

5ml/1 tsp each salt and ground
   black pepper

150g/5oz can tomato purée

250ml/8fl oz/1 cup beer

4 tomatoes, cooked and sieved

350g/12oz/2 cups cooked or
   canned red kidney beans, rinsed
   and drained

salt

To serve

450g/1lb spaghetti, broken in half

250ml/8fl oz/1 cup soured cream

225g/8oz/2 cups grated Cheddar or
   Gruyère cheese

Heat the oil in a deep saucepan and cook the onion and chillies for about 5 minutes, until softened. Add the beef and cook until browned, breaking up the meat with the side of a spoon.

Stir in the garlic, brown sugar, chilli powder, cumin, salt and pepper. Add the tomato purée, beer and sieved tomatoes. Stir to mix. Bring to the boil, then reduce the heat, cover and simmer for 50 minutes.

Stir in the kidney beans and simmer for 5 minutes longer, uncovered.

Meanwhile, cook the spaghetti in a large saucepan of boiling salted water until just tender (check packet instructions for cooking time). Drain.

To serve, put the spaghetti into a warmed bowl. Ladle the chilli over the spaghetti and top with some of the soured cream and grated cheese. Serve the remaining soured cream and cheese separately, if liked.

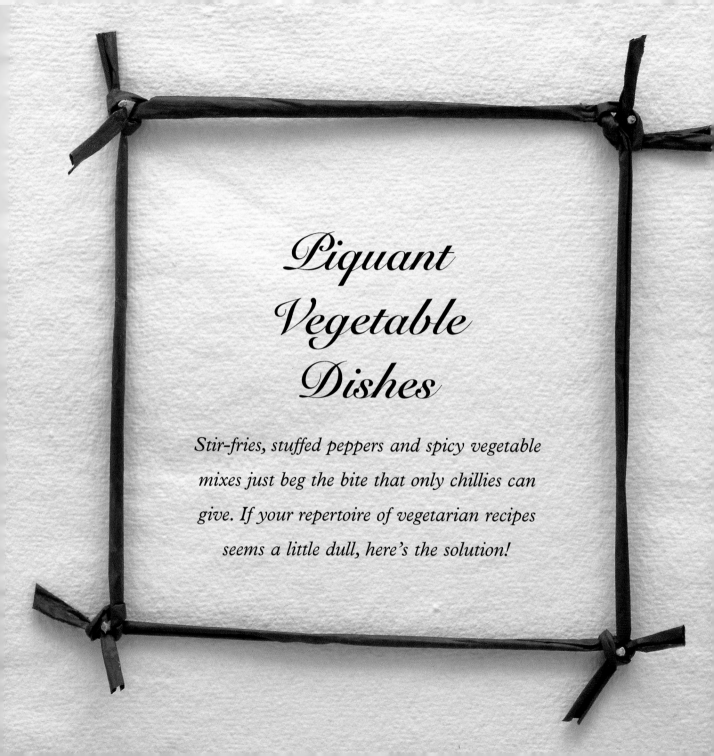

Piquant Vegetable Dishes

Stir-fries, stuffed peppers and spicy vegetable mixes just beg the bite that only chillies can give. If your repertoire of vegetarian recipes seems a little dull, here's the solution!

BEAN CURD AND CHILLI STIR-FRY

Fresh green chillies add a fiery heat to the bean curd and crunchy vegetables in this stir-fry.

Serves 2–4

115g/4oz hard white cabbage

2 fresh green chillies

225g/8oz firm bean curd

45ml/3 tbsp vegetable oil

2 garlic cloves, crushed

3 spring onions, chopped

175g/6oz French beans, trimmed

175g/6oz baby sweetcorn, halved

115g/4oz beansprouts

45ml/3 tbsp smooth peanut butter

25ml/1½ tbsp dark soy sauce

*300ml/½ pint/1¼ cups coconut milk,
   to serve*

COOK'S TIP
*Make sure you buy firm bean
curd which is easy to cut
neatly. Try smoked bean curd
for a change.*

Shred the white cabbage. Carefully remove the seeds and chop the chillies finely. Cut the bean curd into strips.

Heat the wok, then add 30ml/2 tbsp of the oil. When the oil is hot, add the bean curd, stir-fry for 3 minutes and remove with a slotted spoon. Set aside. Wipe out the wok with kitchen paper.

Add the remaining oil to the wok. When it is hot, add the garlic, spring onions and chillies and stir-fry for 1 minute. Add the cabbage, French beans, sweetcorn and beansprouts and stir-fry for a further 2 minutes.

Add the peanut butter and soy sauce and stir to coat. Return the bean curd to the wok, heat through for 1 minute and serve with the coconut milk.

SPICED VEGETABLES WITH COCONUT

This substantial dish, spiced with fresh red chilli, is ideal as a vegetarian main course or as a starter for four.

Serves 2

2 large carrots

6 celery sticks

1 fennel bulb

30ml/2 tbsp grapeseed oil

*2.5cm/1in piece of fresh root ginger,
    peeled and grated*

1 garlic clove, crushed

1 fresh red chilli, seeds removed

3 spring onions, sliced

400ml/14fl oz can thin coconut milk

15ml/1 tbsp chopped fresh coriander

salt and ground black pepper

coriander sprigs, to garnish

Slice the carrots and the celery sticks on the diagonal. Trim the fennel and slice roughly, using a sharp knife. Heat the wok, then add the oil. When the oil is hot, add the ginger, garlic, chilli, carrots, celery, fennel and spring onions. Stir-fry for 2 minutes.

Stir in the coconut milk with a large spoon and bring to the boil. Lower the heat and simmer for 2 minutes. Add the chopped coriander and seasoning to taste. Serve at once, garnished with fresh coriander.

COOK'S TIP
Reserve any green fronds from the fennel bulb to use as a feathery garnish.

POTATOES WITH RED CHILLIES

New potatoes absorb the chilli flavour wonderfully in this fiery-hot, easy-to-make vegetarian dish.

Serves 4

*12-14 new potatoes, scrubbed
    and halved*

30ml/2 tbsp vegetable oil

*2.5ml/½ tsp crushed dried
    red chillies*

2.5ml/½ tsp white cumin seeds

2.5ml/½ tsp fennel seeds

2.5ml/½ tsp crushed coriander seeds

15ml/1 tbsp salt

1 onion, sliced

1-4 fresh red chillies, chopped

15ml/1 tbsp chopped fresh coriander

COOK'S TIP

*Four red chillies may be too
fiery for some palates. For a
milder version, either seed the
chillies, or use fewer.
Experiment with the strength
to find the perfect flavour
balance for your family.*

Bring a saucepan of water to the boil. Add the potatoes and boil for about 15 minutes until tender but still firm. Drain well, return the potatoes to the dry pan and cover with two sheets of kitchen paper to absorb any remaining moisture.

Heat the oil in a deep frying pan, then fry the crushed chillies, all the seeds and the salt for 30–40 seconds over a medium heat.

Add the sliced onion and fry until golden brown. Then add the potatoes, fresh red chillies and fresh coriander. Cover and cook for 5–7 minutes over a very low heat. Serve at once.

CHILLI-STUFFED PEPPERS

This famous Indian dish is made with fresh green chillies. Hot, spicy and extremely delicious, it is best prepared several days in advance with extra oil to allow the spices to mature.

Serves 4–6

15ml/1 tbsp sesame seeds

15ml/1 tbsp white poppy seeds

5ml/1 tsp coriander seeds

60ml/4 tbsp desiccated coconut

½ onion, sliced

2.5cm/1in piece of fresh root
ginger, sliced

4 garlic cloves, sliced

a handful of coriander leaves

6 fresh green chillies

60ml/4 tbsp vegetable oil

2 potatoes, boiled and roughly
mashed

salt, to taste

2 each green, red and yellow peppers

30ml/2 tbsp sesame oil

5ml/1 tsp cumin seeds

60ml/4 tbsp tamarind juice

fresh green chillies, to garnish

In a frying pan, dry-fry the seeds, then add the coconut and continue to roast until it is golden brown. Add the onion, ginger, garlic, coriander and 2 of the chillies and roast for 5 minutes more. Cool, then grind to a paste using a pestle and mortar, food processor or blender. Set aside.

Heat 30ml/2 tbsp of the vegetable oil in the frying pan and fry the ground paste for 4–5 minutes. Add the potatoes and salt and stir well.

Slice the stalk ends off the peppers and reserve for lids. Remove the seeds and any white pith. Fill with the potato mixture and replace the lids.

Heat the sesame oil and remaining vegetable oil in the clean frying pan and fry the cumin seeds and the remaining chillies. When the chillies change colour, add the tamarind juice and bring to the boil. Stand the peppers in the mixture, cover the pan and cook until the peppers are tender. Serve hot or at room temperature, garnished with fresh chillies.

GREEN LIMA BEANS IN CHILLI SAUCE

Colourful and fizzing with flavour, this Mexican vegetable dish uses hot jalapeño chillies.

Serves 4

*450g/1lb green lima or broad beans,
    thawed if frozen*

30ml/2 tbsp olive oil

1 onion, finely chopped

2 garlic cloves, chopped

*3 large tomatoes, peeled, seeded
    and chopped*

*1-2 drained canned jalapeño chillies,
    seeded and chopped*

salt, to taste

fresh coriander sprigs, to garnish

Bring a saucepan of lightly salted water to the boil. Add the beans and cook for 15–20 minutes until tender. Drain and return to the dry pan. Cover tightly to keep the beans hot.

Heat the olive oil in a frying pan and sauté the onion and garlic until the onion is soft but not brown. Add the tomatoes and cook until the mixture is thick and flavoursome. Add the jalapeños and cook for 1–2 minutes. Season with salt.

Pour the mixture over the reserved beans, mix lightly and spoon into a warmed serving dish. Garnish with the coriander and serve.

COOK'S TIP
*Any green beans are delicious
cooked like this. Try Kenyan
fine beans or Egyptian bobby
beans for a change.*

CHILAQUILES

Fried tortilla strips layered with a tomatillo sauce spiced with jalapeños make an unusual vegetarian dish.

Serves 4

60ml/4 tbsp corn or peanut oil

*6 freshly prepared unbaked corn
    tortillas, cut or torn into
    1cm/¹⁄₂in strips*

*275g/10oz can tomatillos (Mexican
    green tomatoes)*

1 onion, finely chopped

*2-3 drained canned jalapeño chillies,
    rinsed, seeded and chopped*

30ml/2 tbsp chopped fresh coriander

*115g/4oz/1 cup grated
    Cheddar cheese*

175ml/6fl oz/³⁄₄ cup vegetable stock

salt and ground black pepper

To garnish

*sliced onion, stuffed green olives and
chopped fresh coriander*

Heat 45ml/3 tbsp of the oil in a large frying pan. Fry the tortilla strips, a few at a time, on both sides, without browning. Add more oil if needed. Drain on kitchen paper.

Put the tomatillos and their juice into a food processor or blender. Add the onion, chillies and coriander. Season with salt and pepper to taste. Process to a smooth purée.

Preheat the oven to 180°C/350°F/Gas 4. Heat the remaining oil in a clean frying pan, add the tomatillo mixture and cook gently for 2–3 minutes, stirring frequently.

Pour a layer of the sauce into the bottom of a shallow baking dish, cover with a layer of tortilla strips, then sprinkle on a layer of grated cheese. Continue layering until all the ingredients have been used, reserving some of the cheese for sprinkling on top.

Pour the vegetable stock over the dish and sprinkle with the reserved cheese. Bake for 30 minutes, or until heated through.

Serve directly from the dish, garnished with sliced onion, stuffed green olives and coriander.

Spicy Salsas, Sauces and Relishes

The role of chillies is to add accent, and these wonderful dips, pickles and salsas do precisely that. For glorious colour and flavour, Chilli and Red Pepper Jelly is the perfect choice.

TOMATO AND CHILLI SALSA

Canned green chillies add zip to this salsa, which is good for livening up grilled meats, fish and shellfish.

Makes 900ml/1½ pints/3¾ cups

1 fresh hot green chilli, chopped

1 garlic clove

½ red onion, roughly chopped

3 spring onions, chopped

*60ml/4 tbsp fresh coriander leaves,
  plus extra, to garnish*

*675g/1½lb ripe tomatoes, seeded and
  roughly chopped*

1-3 drained canned green chillies

15ml/1 tbsp olive oil

30ml/2 tbsp fresh lime or lemon juice

2.5ml/½ tsp salt, or to taste

30-45ml/2-3 tbsp tomato juice

Combine the fresh green chilli, garlic, red onion, spring onions and coriander in a food processor or blender. Process until finely chopped.

Add the tomatoes, canned chillies, olive oil, lime or lemon juice, salt and tomato juice. Pulse until just chopped; the salsa should be chunky.

Transfer to a bowl and taste for seasoning. Cover and leave for at least 30 minutes before serving. This salsa is best served the day it is made. Garnish with coriander.

COOK'S TIP

For less heat, remove the seeds from both the fresh and the canned chillies.

55

SWEET PEPPER AND CHILLI SAUCE

This warming sauce, made with both chilli powder and fresh chilli, is ideal to spice up pasta.

Serves 3-4

30ml/2 tbsp olive oil

1 onion, chopped

1 fresh red chilli, seeded and sliced
(optional)

1 garlic clove, crushed

2 large red or orange peppers, seeded
and finely chopped

5ml/1 tsp chilli powder or sweet
chilli sauce

15ml/1 tbsp paprika

2.5ml/½ tsp dried thyme

225g/8oz can chopped tomatoes

300ml/½ pint/1¼ cups
vegetable stock

2.5ml/½ tsp granulated sugar

salt and ground black pepper

30ml/2 tbsp drained sun-dried
tomatoes in oil, chopped

lettuce, to garnish

freshly cooked pasta, to serve

Heat the oil in a saucepan. Add the onion, fresh chilli (if using), garlic and red or orange peppers. Sauté for 4–5 minutes or until the mixture is lightly browned.

Add the chilli powder or sweet chilli sauce with the paprika and thyme and cook for 1 minute more.

Stir in the tomatoes, vegetable stock and sugar, with salt and pepper to taste. Bring to the boil. Cover, lower the heat and simmer for 20 minutes, adding more stock if necessary.

Stir in the sun-dried tomatoes and cook for 10 minutes or until the tomatoes are tender and the sauce is thick and flavoursome. Serve at once, with freshly cooked pasta, garnished with lettuce.

CHILLI AND COCONUT SALSA

This sweet-and-sour salsa, with the fiery heat of green chillies, goes well with grilled or barbecued fish.

Serves 6–8

1 small coconut

1 small pineapple

2 fresh green chillies

5cm/2in piece of lemon grass

60ml/4 tbsp natural yogurt

2.5ml/ ½ tsp salt

30ml/2 tbsp chopped coriander

coriander sprigs, to garnish

Puncture two of the coconut eyes with a screwdriver and drain the milk from the shell and discard. Crack the coconut shell, prise away the flesh, then coarsely grate the coconut into a bowl.

Cut the rind from the pineapple with a sharp knife and remove the eyes with a potato peeler. Finely chop the flesh and add to the coconut together with any juice from the pineapple.

Cut the chillies in half lengthways and remove the stalks, seeds and membrane. Chop very finely and stir into the coconut mixture.

Finely chop the lemon grass. Stir into the coconut mixture, then add the yogurt, salt and coriander. Mix well. Spoon into a serving dish and garnish with the coriander sprigs. Serve the salsa with grilled or barbecued fish, if you like.

COOK'S TIP

The easiest way to chop the lemon grass is to use a large, sharp cook's knife, placing it at right angles to the cutting surface. Keeping the tip steady, move the handle up and down to shave off fine pieces of lemon grass.

GREEN CHILLI PICKLE

This wonderful pickle comes with a warning, many small green chillies make it extremely hot.

Makes about 675g/1½lb

50g/2oz/½ cup yellow mustard
   seeds, crushed
50g/2oz/½ cup ground cumin
25g/1oz/¼ cup ground turmeric
4 large garlic cloves, crushed, plus
   20 small garlic cloves, peeled and
   left whole
150ml/¼ pint/⅔ cup white vinegar
75g/3oz/¾ cup granulated sugar
10ml/2 tsp salt
150ml/¼ pint/⅔ cup mustard oil
450g/1lb small fresh green chillies,
   halved

COOK'S TIP
*Keep a window open while
cooking with mustard oil as it
is pungent and the smoke may
irritate the eyes.*

Mix the mustard seeds, ground cumin, turmeric, crushed garlic, white vinegar, sugar and salt in a sterilized glass bowl. Cover with a cloth and allow to rest for 24 hours. This enables the spices to infuse and the sugar and salt to dissolve.

Heat the mustard oil in a frying pan and gently fry the spice mixture for about 5 minutes (see Cook's Tip). Add the whole garlic cloves and fry for a further 5 minutes.

Stir in the chillies and cook gently until tender but still green in colour. This will take about 30 minutes over a low heat. Cool thoroughly and pour into sterilized bottles, ensuring the oil is evenly distributed if you are using more than one bottle. Leave to rest for a week before serving.

CHILLI AND GINGER DIP

Red chillies and ginger make up this hot and spicy dip. It is good with vegetables, chicken or seafood.

Makes about 250ml/8fl oz/1 cup

120ml/4fl oz/½ cup sunflower oil

50ml/2fl oz/¼ cup toasted sesame oil

2.5cm/1in piece fresh root
*   ginger, peeled*

1-2 garlic cloves, crushed

2 spring onions, finely chopped

2 red chillies, seeded and
*   finely chopped*

crudités, to serve

COOK'S TIP
Medium-size Mediterranean prawns are ideal served with this sauce. Remove the shell but leave the tails intact so that there is something to hold on to when dipping.

In a small saucepan, gently heat the sunflower oil with the sesame oil. Cut the root ginger into thin slices. Stack the slices and cut them into long thin julienne strips. Turn the strips and cut crossways into very small dice. Put the diced ginger, garlic, spring onions and chillies into the oil. Heat for 5-7 minutes to allow the flavours to infuse. Cool and pour the mixture into a small bowl. Serve with crudités.

CHILLI AND RED PEPPER JELLY

This sweet-savoury jelly, made with red hot chillies, is good with pork, lamb and duck. It would also make an unusual addition to a Ploughman's Lunch, alongside a sharp Cheddar cheese.

Makes about 1.5kg/3–3½lb

1kg/2¼lb eating apples

juice of 1 lemon

1kg/2¼lb/4½ cups granulated sugar

115g/4oz fresh red chillies, seeded and roughly chopped

1 large red pepper, seeded and roughly chopped

1 large Spanish onion, chopped

350ml/12fl oz/1½ cups cider vinegar

COOK'S TIP
Store the jelly in a cool place and it should keep for up to one year.

Cut each apple into about eight pieces, discarding only the bruised and damaged sections, not the cores, peel, seeds or stems. Put into a deep saucepan with the lemon juice and 1 litre/1¾ pints/4 cups cold water. Bring to the boil, lower the heat, cover and simmer for 30 minutes.

Line a colander with a clean dish towel and set it over a deep bowl. Pour the apples and liquid into this and leave to drip through undisturbed.

Discard the apple debris and pour the liquid into a preserving pan with 800g/1¾lb/3½ cups of the sugar. Stir over a low heat until the sugar dissolves completely and the liquid clears. Raise the heat and boil without further stirring until a little of the syrup, spread on a cold plate, wrinkles when you push it with your finger. Start testing after 15 minutes, but anticipate that it may take 30 minutes.

Meanwhile, either mince or process the red chillies, red pepper and onion together to create a fine hash. Scrape the mixture into a large saucepan and stir in the vinegar and remaining sugar. Heat gently until the sugar dissolves, then raise the heat and boil for 5 minutes. Add to the apple syrup and once again boil until the mixture passes the wrinkle test.

Ladle the hot jelly into hot sterilized jars, cover with vinegar-proof discs and lids and cool for about 20 minutes, then turn the jars upside down to redistribute the flecks of pepper. After a further 20 minutes turn them the right way up to complete cooling. Wipe away any external stickiness with a hot damp cloth, then label the jars.